Where's Kendall?

Author: **Kaylen Hawkins**

Illustrator: **Sameer Kassar**

ISBN: 979-8-9861985-0-7 (print book)
979-8-9861985-1-4 (ebook)

DEDICATION

To my sweet, energetic, and adventurous little boy. I can't wait to try to keep up with you for the rest of my life.

A sweet little boy, no older than two, runs around the house finding things to do! Short yet fast and oh so sly, be careful or you'll lose him in the blink of an eye!

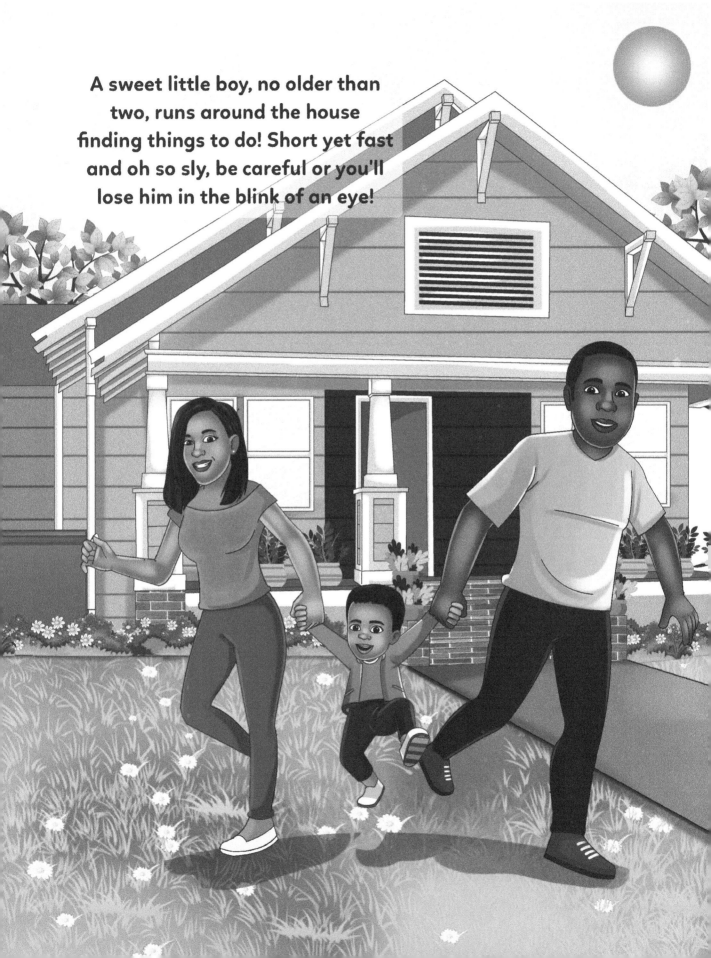

He jumps off the couch as mom picks up a toy. Where did he go?!
That sneaky little boy!

Mom hears a noise as she turns around. A very tiny giggle...a familiar sound.

"Where's Kendall?" she asks as she circles around. "Ah ha I found you in this big blanket mound!"

Around the corner he goes to do something new. Where he ends up I have not a clue! Daddy is cooking and mom goes upstairs. Kendall runs around without any worries or cares.

Daddy hears a noise as he chops up some food.
That same little giggle in that happy little mood.

"Where's Kendall?" he asks as he looks to the right. Hands in the freezer holding onto the ice cream so tight!

Daddy takes it from him and as quick as a fox, in a few steps he's at his toy box.

Kendall looks down low to see what's inside. Where is his new car? Is it trying to hide? He stretches out an arm but it's way too far! He falls in the toy box trying to grab that car!

"Where's Kendall?" he asks as he walks up behind. "Silly boy. What have you gotten into this time? Here's your car, now Daddy has to cook. Why don't you come look for a good book?"

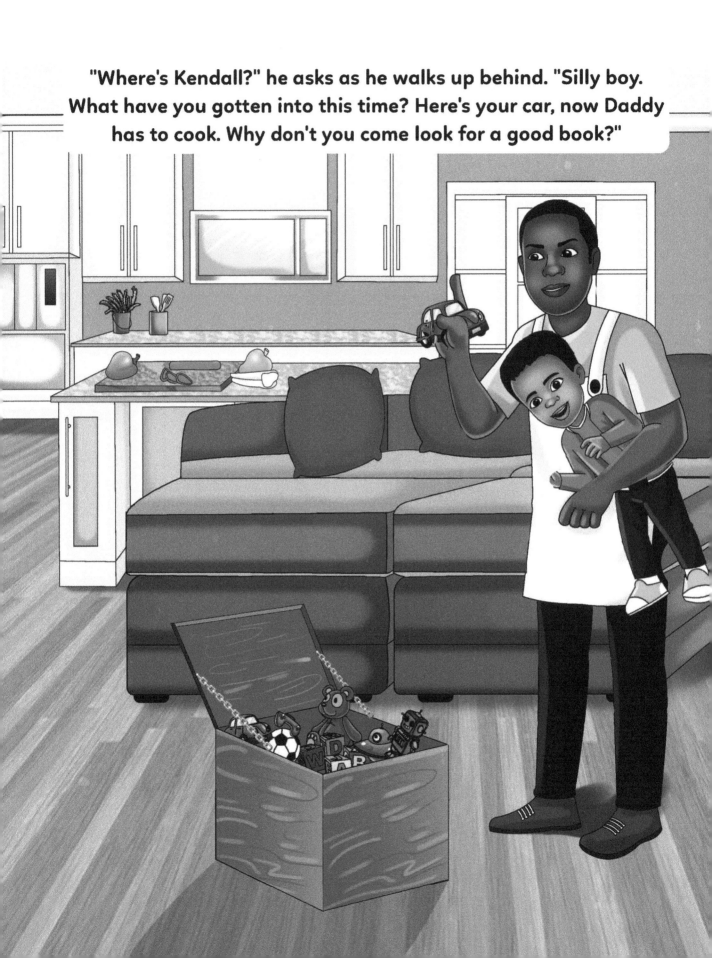

He sits down to read but it doesn't last long.

Daddy hears a flush....oh no what's wrong?

That cheerful giggle is what Daddy hears, but with the flush of a toilet it's accompanied by fears. "Where's Kendall?" He asks as he heads towards the sound. "Drop it!" he says as the book quickly falls down.

"Come here." Daddy says. "Let's close this door. Go to your blanket and sit on the floor. I hear Mommy coming. She will read to you. Something you always like to do!"

Mommy takes the book and puts Kendall in her lap. They read the story with all the peek-a-boo flaps. "Good job, Baby." Mommy says when they are finally done. "Go upstairs with me so you can have some more fun."

Mommy grabs the hamper and that pair of dirty socks.
Kendall is in the corner playing with his blocks. Mommy turns
around to grab a bib. Then she hears a slight giggle coming
from over by the crib.

"Where's Kendall?" she asks as she goes across the room. "Did the hamper eat him? Did he meet his doom?" Kendall smiles as the hamper is lifted off, he rises and runs. He hasn't had enough!

Mom picks up the clothes and walks down the hall. She turns the corner and hears a giggle-like call. "Where's Kendall?" she asks as she peeks in the door. He's staring out the window, his tiptoes on the floor.

"Wait here while I take the dry clothes out. Be patient, please do not cry or pout."

"Where's Kendall?" she asks as she looks inside. "I see he's found a new place to hide." In the dryer trying to close the door. Having so much fun and looking for more.

"Out you go my silly little boy. Go play with one or ALL of your toys!" Kendall puts his feet on the laundry room floor, gets a running start and heads for the door. Through the closet and to the next place, a bounce in his step and a smile on his face.

Mommy finishes her task and turns the machine on, no more than a minute was she even gone. That same little giggle floats to her ear. Where oh where is her little dear?

On his little horse but standing on his feet! It's his bottom that should be in that seat! "Kendall, why are you up so high? Come here now." Mommy said with a sigh.

Mommy takes him down and holds him close. "You know it's you I love the most. Curious and adventurous you will always be. It helps you to learn; that's what I see. Take your time and learn in stride. Mommy and Daddy will be along for the ride."

The End

About the Author

Kaylen Hawkins, author of "Where's Kendall" is a daughter, sister, wife, and mother living in North Carolina. A native of Greensboro, she received her Bachelor of Science and Master's Degrees in Communication Sciences and Disorders at the University of North Carolina at Chapel Hill. She is currently a licensed Speech Language Pathologist working in Guilford County school system. Her favorite job by far is being a Mommy to her toddler Kendall. She hopes that writing this storybook will allow parents of curious and energetic children to better embrace their young one's adventurous nature and attempt to turn curiosity into positive learning experiences!

9 798986 198507